THE PORTAGE POETRY SERIES

I0542963

Series Titles

New Wilderness
Jenifer DeBellis

Silent Letter
Gail Hanlon

Bowed As If Laden With Snow
Megan Wildhood

Always a Body
Molly Fuller

Fulgurite
Catherine Kyle

The Body Is Burden and Delight
Sharon White

Bone Country
Linda Nemec Foster

Not Just the Fire
R.B. Simon

Monarch
Heather Bourbeau

The Walk to Cefalù
Lynne Viti

The Found Object Imagines a Life: New and Selected Poems
Mary Catherine Harper

Naming the Ghost
Emily Hockaday

Mourning
Dokubo Melford Goodhead

Messengers of the Gods: New and Selected Poems
Kathryn Gahl

After the 8-Ball
Colleen Alles

Careful Cartography
Devon Bohm

Broken On the Wheel
Barbara Costas-Biggs

Sparks and Disperses
Cathleen Cohen

Holding My Selves Together: New and Selected Poems
Margaret Rozga

Lost and Found Departments
Heather Dubrow

Marginal Notes
Alfonso Brezmes

The Almost-Children
Cassondra Windwalker

Meditations of a Beast
Kristine Ong Muslim

Praise for
New Wilderness

"With emotional poise and lyrical splendor Jenifer DeBellis recreates glass-sharp details and images of a mother always in rescue mode, and her eldest daughter, who, since infancy, lived in gripping persistent need. 'It's more like you're air-/ traffic control and she's hijacked a plane/ she has no idea how to navigate.' The real splendor of this book is in the variety of beautifully crafted poetic forms; poems which themselves are objects of rescue, for they bring order to all the contextual turmoil. I could not put this book of valorous verse down."

—Joy Gaines-Friedler
author of *Capture Theory*

"'Truth is, the world's sold you a lie …' Jenifer DeBellis becomes a myth-breaker as, with bracing honesty, she complicates the figures of the precious child, the 'warrior mom,' the good doctor, and the inspirational cancer survivor. Yes, this collection has fortitude and resilience in spades, but DeBellis arrives at these only after meticulously surveying the wreckage that illness makes of good intentions, the individual self, and family trust. Not an easy read, *New Wilderness*, but one that pushes us to see behind 'Insta-perfect shots by the Ferris wheel backlit by an electric/ sunset' and leaves us with a blueprint for bearing the slings and arrows of any human life."

—Iain Haley Pollock
author of *Ghost, like a Place*

"Readers of *New Wilderness* witness the human strength of a mother and the bravery of a poet confronting spaces where 'Nothing you say makes any of / it go away, any of it // better.' DeBellis's use of image, humor and irony (always in tune with contemporary speech) allows readers to navigate emotional highs and lows of mental/physical health as a survivor would and, hopefully, understand the unique power of women, of mothers and of poetry."

—Brad Johnson
author of *Smuggling Elephants Through Airport Security*

New Wilderness

poems

Jenifer DeBellis

Cornerstone Press
Stevens Point, Wisconsin

Cornerstone Press, Stevens Point, Wisconsin 54481
Copyright © 2023 Jenifer DeBellis
www.uwsp.edu/cornerstone

Printed in the United States of America by
Point Print and Design Studio, Stevens Point, Wisconsin

Library of Congress Control Number: 2023933356
ISBN: 978-1-960329-01-1

Cornerstone Press titles are produced in courses and internships offered by the
Department of English at the University of Wisconsin–Stevens Point.

DIRECTOR & PUBLISHER   EXECUTIVE EDITOR
Dr. Ross K. Tangedal   Jeff Snowbarger

SENIOR EDITORS
Lexie Neeley, Monica Swinick, Kala Buttke

PRESS STAFF
Ellie Atkinson, Patrick Fogarty, Angela Green, Jordan Hansen, Cal Henkens,
Brett Hill, Julia Kaufman, Amanda Leibham, Cat Scheinost, Maria Scherer, Taylor
Schmidt, Cash Van Stiphout, Matt Vancik, Abbi Wasielewski

To Catrina,
who's been a remarkable character
since she entered the world
like a launched rocket,
knowing how to fly
before her first cry.

Also by Jenifer DeBellis:

Warrior Sister, Cut Yourself Free from Your Assault
Blood Sisters

Poems

After the Rain

Swept into the tempo of "Only Happy
When It Rains," you crank the volume.

In the gutter space where Shirley Manson
needs your misery to pour down,
needs your misery to pour down on her,[1]
you glimpse the storm that rages within
your daughter's broken soul caged by conflict.

Yet, unlike the song, her soul's comfort
is the night turned bright. Where there's nothing
to pull from the shadows, she'll use
what's within reach to cast shadow
puppets in skits against memory's backlit wall.

Do not be deceived when she says
she hates drama. Her survival depends on
turmoil-churned storms that fuel
the tropical cyclone's rapid rotations.

She's learned it's the time
just after the storm, when rain & wind
wane, that the rescue mission begins.
She knows there's no relief
effort without casualties & devastation.

She's spent so much time in the storm
eye, though, she no longer sees
where the storm ends & she begins.
She sucks in surface air to feed
her inner fire. The broken soul forgets
she's after what follows the rain,

forgets how to escape
her own self-destructive path.

Manic Moments

Since her 1st birthday you recognize your daughter's mania
as more than tantrums & mood swings she'll outgrow

with more tough love & textbook care. Loved ones criticize
your lack of control, offer to keep her for a week & break her

bad behavior & spirit. *Inappropriate* is a label used to mark
her mistimed sadness, desire, elation, anxiety & anger.

Her racing mind out runs her energy highs. Try to keep up
with her hastened speech & tone, or her epic vision

of reality. Her cognitive skills are advanced for her age.
Her memory keener. By 3 she beats you in memory games

designed for 5 & up. By 4 she looks & acts 6. By grade
school she's disengaged: *nothing interests me anymore*

she says. Her teen years are fogged with miscalculated
hormone therapies & the GI disease these provoke.

She's 18 when a state clinician offers psych meds
& validates her lifelong battle to attain a normal life

her misfiring mind could never reach with more effort
or refining alone. Alone is a love-hate concept she adopts.

I'm so alone | Leave me alone | I don't want to be alone

You'll learn—like you learned as a child—to measure her
moods against weather patterns lurking in a hidden realm

only your 6th sense can discern. You'll become a well-
trained service pet that senses & calms her imminent

attacks before you're all swept into flash flood rapids
that are no respecter of person, property, or destination.

Precious Girl

At three months old, she spoke
her first word. *Hi* she cooed back
when you craned in close

& said, *Hi. Hi, my precious girl,*
Hi drawn out in your singsong
tone. Mimicry was her second gift—

her first was her love of sleep.
She spoke in complete sentences
by eleven months. *I want*

was her favorite phrase. *I want.*
I want that. No, give me that,
she'd say, extending her tiny hands.

Read to me. Sing to me. Sit with me.
You were her chosen performer
& pal. As social as she was

with you, she had issues with others.
Wouldn't stay where you weren't
present. Then, temper tantrums

when it was time to follow rules
or stop playtime. Another mom
told you about Mom & Tots

held at the community center.
Said, *the teacher's a miracle*
worker. So you joined.

Your daughter & you were sent
into the hallway for timeouts
all but two minutes of the one-hour

session. Alone again in the hall,
no longer able to hide
your shame or pit stains,

you hissed, *What's wrong
with you?* She shook her head,
her sad brown eyes drooped

in defeat. *I don't know.*
But you brought her back
the next week since you paid

& prayed for a miracle. This time
you only spent half the session
in the hall. By the third visit,

only two timeouts. & so it went
for eight weeks. The last day
the teacher said, *I didn't think*

you'd be back after that first class.
Or second. In my thirty years
as a teacher I've never met

a more dedicated mother.
You nodded thanks because
your tongue was wrapped

around a sob. Determined,
you thought, but not dedicated.
That's a word reserved

for those whose pure thoughts
are free of dreaded visions
where they're imprisoned

behind the rest of a day
that has them inventing new ways
to reach their unrefined child.

Come For Your Girl

Moonlight refracts from her tear-
streaked cheeks. *Another nightmare?*

you ask. Her tiny forehead tenses.
Her almond eyes widen. *The glow-eyed*

grey girl is back? Through quivering lips
she sobs, *She never leaves.* You know this

terror, know the way night carves
an opening into your world

after the sun burns out & all the lights
in the house grow cold.

All you can do is help her
take back her space—claim authority

over this power of darkness
that's followed you from your childhood

& now comes nightly for your girl.
She spider-hugs you as you carry her

back to her bedroom, where the nightlight
has gone out. Despite the pricked skin

fear you now share, you tread barefoot
past the nursery for a replacement bulb.

She's gripped so tight to your neck,
your throat constricts but you don't

complain. It's a small price you pay
to break an isolation cycle

that was never enough to snuff
your *make-believe fears & monsters.*

Safely back in her bed,
you cast shadow puppets overhead.

Her head cradled in your elbow crook,
your left fingertips pressed to her right,

you itsy, bitsy spider crawl
across the ceiling, rain-wash her fears

away until sunrise helps you
both climb back into slumber.

Early Patterns

A wild goose never laid a tame egg.

—Gaelic proverb

1. Tia used to line up figures according to size
    & color. Largest to smallest—the larger closest

    to the castle or barn entrance. Sometimes
    they rode the Lucky Duck conveyer this way.

    Big Bird, horse, cow, pig, duck, cowboy,
    chicken, Piglet, duck, Pooh, swan, Elmo, duck.

    Princess Aurora—Tia's middle name—waited
    alone in the fenced-in yard. *Wouldn't Aurora*

    in pink fit better than Elmo? you asked once.
    Or watching her kingdom from the balcony?

    No, she said. *She doesn't fit in with them.*

2. She colored in repeating rainbow patterns:
    purple, blue, green, yellow, orange, red, pink.

    Coloring book characters wore rainbows
    in worlds that shared the same spectrum palette.

    When a color was missing, she mixed her own
    or formed new patterns. To distinguish things

    she altered the diagonal design direction.
    She began dressing herself in rainbow patterns.

    Then insisted you & her little sis did the same.

3.   She carried the patterns into her Barbie phase.
Dressed in their daytime best, Barbies & Kens

hung out at the dinner table or in the living room.
They sat girl girl boy girl girl boy with one

girl left alone in another room. Sometimes
when you cleaned up toys after she fell asleep

you moved the loner girl to the hangout spot.
Yet she was back on her own by morning.

You were grateful when the isolation
period ended. Even though there were now

boy girl pairs that bared their naked bodies.

Unwelcome Foe

It's hard to find redeeming traits about her
sweet 16 party. Her friend bash followed
the family celebration—the first
to include boys. A tiki torch path led
guests to the bonfire out back. Kids became
carloads of young adult tailgaters, who trailed
in & filled half your six-acre estate.
Things out back got lit while you patrolled
& cleared the front yard of uninvited guests.
When an unwelcome foe showed up wasted,
you had her taken home where Mom, as texts
warned, called the cops to say she was roofied—
despite knowing she stole her brother's meds
& a fifth of vodka. Most kids scattered
into the woods by the time the cop showed
up—your daughter included. Empty
Coke cans & a lone beer burned in the pit.
The cop fined minors & you for hosting
an underage drinking party despite
your compliance & evidence showing
otherwise. You spent the next year fighting
to prove your innocence while they used you
to scare the other parents in town who
did host parties that condoned teen drinking.

Detroit Institute of Arts

You don't talk anymore.
She's too angry & you can't seem
to find middle ground.

So you text each other.
Even today at the DIA
she texts you

it should be a crime to
drag someone to a place
like this against their will

Her will, you mean.
You might enjoy it.

not a chance -_-

So you walk in a silence
that blankets your life
like a volatile storm cloud
looking for a landscape
to unleash its full fury.

You stop in front of van Gogh's
Bank of the Oise at Auvers,
tugging her arm to tether her
to one spot for a change.

See it?
the way the trees sway?

She rolls her eyes, blows
her bangs from her forehead.

you forgot to cap your t

it must take a lot of talent
to paint thin men

What about this one?

You stop in front of van Gogh's
Self Portrait with Straw Hat.

van gagme

Seriously, look at the
detail, the dimension in
the brushstrokes

It's clear the gallery attendant
following you is uncomfortable
with your closeness to the art.

I wish I could touch this
one—run my hand along
his jaw.

straw man in straw hat
hawt

You keep moving;
it's what you both do well.
You point out *Eleonora
of Toledo and Her Son.*

lady in a rug with her
creepy chucky doll son

It's Bronzino's adaptation
of Madonna & Child.

let the nightmares begin

Maybe this *was* a bad idea.

You wander aimlessly now.
No longer point
or pause to share. You turn
to her; it's time
to raise the white flag.

But she's stopped
in the gallery center,
her chin thrust
to the octagonal heaven
of Tintoretto's
The Dreams of Men.

Wow, she says,
her arms limp
at her sides, her jaw slack.

I know, you say back, no
desire to look away
from her enchanted face.

More Than You Want to Deal With

Where she wavered with her own life
& death   wishes   she fought
to preserve life   in all forms

around her   It's why she studied
to be a CNA & plans to become a nurse
Her heart breaks into action for the suffering

One night   she nudged you awake
at 3am   there was a tremor in her
plea for you to come quietly a faint cry

on the other side of her door   revealed
this might be more than she knew
you wanted to deal with   *Don't be mad*

I couldn't leave him behind that barn to die

It was young & frantic   You sensed this
               was big & there was that wild cry
still calling to you   You weren't prepared

for the skeletal kitten that stood
on the bed's edge   His awkward long legs
trembled   His eyes fevered with fear

like a child clinging to wakefulness through
a nightmare-filled slumber   *Help me
Mom*   she begged   *I can't get him to shut up*

While you held your daughter   & caressed
the kitten till his shudders & mews subsided

you thought about your own mom who never
held you this way   who didn't know how

As both gangly-legged babies slept
you wondered how many times
          your sixteen-year-old
mom   thought   about saying
Don't be mad   Mom   Help me

          while her secret swelled
within her   threatening to give you away

New Wilderness

Picture this, it's a quiet Friday morning. You sip
your second cup of coffee while a cackle
of crows pester a Red-tailed Hawk, driving it

from snow-dressed ash branch to ash branch
in the marsh out back. Your view through this glass
wall is picturesque. The sun's out for the first time

in weeks. Frosted tufts of Indian grass & hardstem
bulrush glisten as they reach skyward like winter
has hardly bitten them. This view's what sold you

on the house you've spent two decades making
into a home—a fact you point out to your spouse

who lounges across from you. Your phone vibrates
mid-sentence with a call from your daughter
who's at college four states away. *Are you alone?*

she asks once you return her hi. *No, I'm with Dad.*
Good, she says, *I have bad news. They found*
an astrocytoma glioma on my right frontal lobe.

Your breath constricts. *In English*, you demand,
though you know she's about to say brain tumor.

You stare through the pane, past the bleak lawn
until your eyes settle on the wilderness beyond.

Barren Michigan maples, white pines & oak
trunks blur into a tangled shadow. You think
she's just said surgery is set for next month

but you can't find your way out of the shifting
tree trunk labyrinth now caging you in.

Sometime between shock & anger, you find your way
to her pre-op bedside, where talk turns to advance
directives & complications. *Surgery was a success*,

the neurosurgeon beams when he finds you curled
in a lounge chair, watching the sun rise over
the rolling horizon of the Blue Ridge Mountains.

What you'll soon learn is surgery was the easy part.
Memory loss, mood swings & relearning will fog
the days that precede radiation + chemo.

Nothing you do quells her headaches & heartaches.
Nothing you say makes any of it go away, any of it

better. Yet between prescription pick-ups & inventing
new ways to braid her hair to hide her scar & hair loss,
you make sure she eats, has clean sheets, remembers

to shower & brush her teeth. Then treatment begins
& you're reminded—as she grows weaker, sleeps
whole days without waking, turns her resentment

toward you—none of it is enough or makes a real
difference. But you do it anyway because
your own healing comes from this simple service

you're able to offer her. You're sure she hates you,
hates that you can't make it all better like you did
when she skinned her knees or had a nightmare.

You know this because you know that look
she gives you when you ask what else you can do.
It's the look she used through her teenage years

to let you know you've ruined things *again*,
that you always ruin everything. So you back away,

find an escape like you learned to do when
her inner fears morph into outward frustration.

There's a private lake path you discovered
on a previous hike. It's a comfort place

you return to when your head clogs with regret,
with deferred hope, with your own frustration.

As you walk, you're enveloped in hemlocks,
birches & halesia trees, their newly bloomed
silverbell clusters burst from over-dressed branches.

You compete with Cackling Geese & their goslings
for your share of the path. You envy their simple life,
their determined ways. Recall when your own days

could be simplified to keeping your little ones in line
& the resolute focus such simplicity required.

You marvel over how prepared you were to witness
each growth, each milestone. How ready—excited
even—you were to watch your girls' wings unfurl

as they entered the world, their bright lives ahead
of them. You realize, dodging dung droppings,

how unprepared you are for your daughter's
uncertain journey. This new waiting burrows a hole

in your visions of her future. This new waiting
has a name you cannot name, fills your focus

with an endless wait there's no preparing for.
You welcome it just as you welcomed a life by faith.

Though, given a choice, you'd not answer this call.

Mixed Blessings

Her cosmos shifts as she collides head on with an open cabinet, rushing to make it to work on time. The door's bottom corner stabs her above the right temple. A retrograde rotation knocks her out. Galactic photon flashes blur her vision, cloud her morning drive. She's orbited this realm many times, knows the warning signs of a concussion & checks herself into the ER before her own shift in 3 Central. Tests & x-ray confirm her suspicions. Her inner axis doesn't realign during recovery. Dark matter loosed from hiding, her headaches redouble—morph into a pulsing ache unlike the ones she's nursed a lifetime. The new ENT suggests another sinus surgery & requests a CT. Neurology follows up with her after the radiologist compares her new scans with those taken five years ago back home.

Why'd your office call me back instead of the ENT? she asks.
Because your tumor has grown, the caller says.   *What tumor?*

Bruised Lifeline

You watch her neuro-ICU bedside
    monitor, absence of flatline
    your prayer. Heartrate, BP,
    oxygen, intercranial pressure
    readings scratch a new asterism
    across the LCD. Glass
    to sand to glass again—her
    quartz reflection shines
    celestial from the screen.
    Her matrix face hides
    behind rogue waves in neon
    lime, pomegranate, blueberry
    & plum. You can almost taste
    the space these new lines carve
    into your daughter's bruised lifeline.

Try to Imagine

A kiss is a lovely trick, designed by nature,
to stop words when speech becomes unnecessary.

—Ingrid Bergman

They wean her from her post-op coma
but can't stabilize her pain or nausea.

The only pain med she doesn't throw up
is liquid Tylenol they feed her IV. *But*

I can't keep authorizing that for you,
the weekend attending says during rounds.

There's a shortage of liquid drugs
since the hurricane hit Puerto Rico.

I can only prescribe these in emergencies.
You try to imagine what's more

an emergency than a swelling brain
under trauma as the doctor flees

the room as quickly as he entered.
We're working on it, her nurse says,

handing your daughter a Tylenol-3
she refuses after vomiting the last

two doses within minutes. *Please*,
she pleads, *it aggravates my head*

to puke & you know about my gastroparesis.

You kiss her hand between massaging
it. When she pulls it away

you lean over the bed rail & kiss her
temple like you once did in her crib

& at your breast when she fell away
content & subdued by peaceful rest.

You hope your kisses deliver
a shot of oxytocin to her brain,

help ease her anxiety & stress
like they did during panic attacks.

Let a serotonin infusion offset
her cortisol levels so she sleeps

through this conscious nightmare.

Mirror, Mirror

Hours after surgery, the right side
of her face swells & morphs her

into the monster she once feared
had climbed through the attic door

& hid in her closet. They told you
this would happen but what can

prepare you for this deformed face
that's mangled your first baby's

appearance? You keep your own
face relaxed, despite the knots

in your gut & thoughts. She grew
up a Disney princess. Knew all

the words to *The Little Mermaid*
& *Snow White. Where's my mirror,*

she says between swollen lips?
You should wait, you say. Though

you hand it to her anyway because
you know she won't let it go.

She pulls the mirror overhead first,
then lowers it so she's eye-to-eye

with this wicked version of herself.
It'll get better, you say. This brings

you back to those other times
she needed you to make her feel

beautiful & you did, needed you to tell her
she'd be okay, that she'd survive

& somehow she did. It was easy
to say these things & mean it when

the stakes were small, trivial even.
She raises the mirror again. Then drops

her hands. When she looks at you
her good eye waters. She waits

for you to finish with *You'll survive.*

Braiding Your Daughter's Hair After Brain Surgery

When she asks you to fix her
hair, you will dig deep into creativity,
keep your hands steady, your breath even.
She waits for your reaction to her
butchered skull—knows you hate gore, hate to see
her suffer even more. You stare down at her
shaved scar. Metal staples poke from her swollen scalp.
It's not that bad, you say, eyeing her
in the mirror she holds as you work.

Her brow is pinched & you know
the head pounding is peaking. But
there's another hour until her next round of pain
meds. You loose blood scabs from her hair
strand-by-strand because every strand counts,
then weave small sections into a braid
screen that will fool anyone who doesn't know
better. Even she's impressed. For a moment,
you're grateful for the smile you catch on her worn face.

[Re]Naming Things

When she was young she insisted on naming things with native words. *Come si dice [ ] in Italiano* is a game you played to learn new words.

She'd kick & scream when she didn't get her way. In a thundercloud of clashing wills, you rode out her storms so she could learn new words.

In school her peers teased her, said she'd never escape your small town. So she built her career, cut ties & relocated to teach them new words.

She called to share her diagnosis: a C word you didn't dare say aloud. You refused to name it, though she was still forced to know new words.

They drilled a hole to sever tumor & memories. The void is a phantom limb where recall backfires & means she must (re)learn new words.

She learned her loss was vast; entire conversations & concepts had been wrenched from her past. How can she reclaim these as new words?

Words aren't all she lost. She lost years on her lifespan & two years in her studies. *Hope* & *desire deferred* are a few of her new words.

Come si dice *I'm nothing* in Italiano? Come si dice *what's it matter anymore*? Tia asks. & here's where you refuse to teach her new words.

Small, Dark Spaces

When she was twelve, she folded herself in half
& hid in a cedar trunk during *Hide & Seek*. The oldest
among the kids, she knew the others would never
think to check this hiding spot. She was right.
A dozen minutes later & the kids lost interest—
abandoned the game for the swing set out back.
She was almost out of air when she pressed the top
& found it latched shut. You eventually heard her
screams as moms tend to do. Found her locked
away & rescued her from that attic bedroom.

She never outgrew her fear of small, dark spaces.
Between surgery & radiation + chemo, she recalls
this memory. Confesses she wishes you could
rescue her from the dungeon in her disheveled head.

First Radiation Treatment

You can't imagine what she feels
after she hops onto the bed deck,
fits her custom mesh mask
over her face & lies back to align
her head with the gantry mouth.
Stay still so the laser can do its job,
the tech reminds her. *Ten minutes,*
in & out. Then he feeds her
to the machine. When he'd handed
her the mask, her eyes told you
what she refused to say: *I'm afraid.*
Afraid of small, dark spaces. Afraid
this new hurt will be my undoing.
Afraid this won't work. Afraid of how
long ten minutes are when I'm alone,
measuring my fear of defeat,
of a slow death like the ones I watch
my own patients suffer when radiation
& chemo rounds chew the life from
their bodies but leave behind disease.

I'll be waiting for you on the other side
of the window, you say, afraid
she has seen your mirrored fears flash
before you secure your own mask.

Fighting for Her

The oldest of three daughters
she's the one   who forces you

to be warrior mom   master calmer
defender of secret fears
            & rescuer from impossible

problems   She tells you
she lives for you   does chemo
& radiation for you   The hormones

& harvested eggs   that's right
all for you too   Says she stopped

fighting to live for herself   long
before brain surgery   & you know
this truth   You've been fighting

for her since she was born   Even
held her twice through sweat-soaked
nights of convulsions after you pressed

your fingers down her throat & delivered
the bottle of pills she'd   swallowed

Checking In Instead of Out

Problem was, before they found the tumor,
her mental unraveling frayed the edges of her
routines. She worked harder to link tasks
to their respective actions. But those around her
assumed she'd simply burned out, grown slack
with the stretching such nursing programs
are known for. It's how they weed out the weak.

Problem was, the directors & dean collected to fix
her fate the day before finals: a push to withdraw.
She fought them until she saw it their way.
One day remaining, she played the only viable card
they dealt her: a mental emergency withdrawal.

Problem was, she was sedated when she called
you from the observation clinic. Said she was on
voluntary watch for a mandatory three days. Then
said she must cut herself from the outside world
so she could tame the insanity eroding her mind.

Problem was, you've seen this madness before
in your child's eyes, seen darkness consume her
pupils till the only light left was the chaos
glinting through a roadmap of expanded blood
vessels that graphed the way to her personal hell.

Problem was, how could you know the pressure
in her right frontal lobe was in control of her
impaired emotions & behavior? How could anyone
know for five years her brain had been feeding
a tumor that fueled her drive, inhibitions & moods?

Problem was, five years prior, a radiologist
& neurologist dismissed her tumor without telling
you about it. Said in the notes the new neurologist

reviewed, her CT imaging & evaluations
showed astrocytoma >5cm. Their diagnosis:
unknown cause for her mini stroke episode.

Problem was validated when her clinical instructor
saw her name on the neuro post-op patient board
while doing rounds with students. Sent her flowers
& sent the dean a note, explaining the destiny
of that student they weeded out for mental weakness.

Asylum

Her thoughts are a graffiti of spontaneous phrases
& lines. Her mind's four walls of clipped

& looped words left by hasty hands. One door, no
windows, the only light a hanging bare bulb.

> *I'm in hell*
> *help me*

someone's written on a wall. Above this reads

> *One word in a hand*
> *is worth more than*
> *six behind sealed lips.*

To fall asleep she beats her head
into the stripped mattress, ignoring

the stench of stale bile. She leaves a light on
to fight off her fears. When she changes

her sweat-soaked tee or gets off to fill
the static silence, she senses someone

watching. She tries to forget this
but her feelings fall like rain, overwhelm

like runoff water rushing past clogged
gutters, rage through restless nights,

settle at her feet in stagnant pools
with nowhere to go. She's ready to write.

> *There is no hell*
> *like this room in my head*
> *no light enough*
> *to lead the way out*

Mental Ruins

The remains of her mental framework protrude
from her crumbled mind
the way a carcass does
long after its flesh has decayed.

From her crumbled mind
light refracts from a metallic surface.
Long after its flesh has decayed
& rains have washed the blubber clean,

light refracts from a metallic surface.
Her memories were vibrant loom bracelets
& rains have washed the rubber clean.
This scene is inescapable, & real.

Her memories were vibrant loom bracelets
& this is the nightmare she relives as they dig.
This scene, it's inescapable. & real
are the threats that force memories into hiding.

& this is the nightmare she relives as they dig:
lessons, once learned, now unsoldered
are the threats that force memories into hiding.
Their absence sings a soul song her heart's forgotten.

Lessons, once learned, now unsoldered
to reveal a war-torn playground. Void of kid song,
their absence stings. A soul song her heart's forgotten
becomes a phantom limb without autonomy.

To reveal a war-torn playground void of kid song,
the road to memory's demolished until it
becomes a phantom limb without autonomy.
Is it better to never know than forget

the road to memories? Demolished until it
loses its way to the brain, she says,
Is it better to never know than forget?
In this restless desert place, identity

loses its way, too. *My brain*, she says,
is sand keeping time in severed glass bulbs.
In this restless desert place, identity
loss is a fear that mirrors your own.

Is sand keeping time? Severed glass bulbs
is this new landscape & now
loss is a fear that mirrors your own
thoughts. No longer whole

is this new landscape. & now
she's begun to unhinge . . .
thoughts, no longer whole,
turned rubble of shrapnel, scrap glass, rock.

She's begun to unhinge
the way a carcass does.
Turned rubble of shrapnel, scrap glass, rock,
the remains of her mental framework protrude.

Red Tide at Dusk

You refuse to let a little toxic air come between you guys
& your night out. The beachfront sign reads, *no swimming:*
Karenia brevis concentrations. Like *Katrina,* waves beat
the beach. Winds skim the shore & kick up algal bloom
that constricts your breath intake. Several guests leave
before their food arrives, their collars pulled up to cover
their mouths. You fold over a few times as you walk
the pier that leads to patio seating, your throat & eyes seal
in resistance to the poison. You can't catch your breath
like you couldn't catch it as a kid when trouble whipped
up around you with little warning. This time is different
between child & parents, though. Your conversation breaks

the surface as the sun hits the horizon. The least adapted to red
tide, you take longer to loosen your lungs & find your voice.

Surfing Darkness

After body surfing evening's post storm wake,
your waterlogged bodies lie beached where waves break
the shoreline. Four chins to sand, tide rolls over
your backs & washes razor clams ashore. You adore

these three unique versions of yourself at different
ages. Five years separate them like the five years
that separated the tumor's discovery & disclosure.
Seaweed & red drift algae cling to your sticky skin

but the clams that rode waves to shore burrow
into sand until buried. They disappear below wet
darkness you know well—an underworld the oldest
discovered long before her tumor formed.

When the tide recedes, trademark   dents   pock
the beach, giving away the clams' hiding places.
They don't know to erase their trail any more
than your daughters knew their shadows revealed

them hidden behind drapes. You often let them
believe you couldn't find them   just to hear
the giggles that followed their sly realization
they beat you—you whose eyes were all-knowing.

Sun-kissed, golden shells, the clams' oblong shape
mimics an aerial view of a sandbar just before dusk
tucks it in for the night. You can't help but note
the maritime dangers sandbanks impose on those

places coastal waters meet alcoves. Nor the perils
that pricked your skin at the tumor's second discovery
& its first disclosure. Nothing softens the blow
that experts five years ago knew about this saltwater

pearl size tumor, now triple this size. The clam's
razor edges are immovable, hinged shut
like your daughter's skull before they burrow
a hole in it & pry open this dark hiding spot.

What ugliness lurks in this secret chamber?
There won't be precious pearls.   No beauty
will form from years of layered defenses
against parasites. Her eroded thoughts are plankton

too mentally weak to swim against currents
that rush her toward this skull-wrecked moment.
Time between discovery & disclosure has sifted
through an hourglass now three-quarters drained.

Experts have flipped the glass. Sand now slips
madly back onto itself as if to bury alive the child.

The ocean shushes competing voices that ripple
around a C word usually reserved for adults
you know. Then, this momentary calm recedes
& chaos floods your intertidal thought zone.

How will she weather these after storm waters?
How will you
                    help her stay above the waves?

Static Chaos

Post-op, isolation strikes her. She's a starling

pitched from its flock in flight, now
dropped ashore to forever wander aimlessly.

Her life, now confined to a vacant chamber.
An attic space. A place of neglected

& abandoned things. Of forgotten effects,
some that can never be removed, not

even by a neurosurgeon's skilled hands.
True to its nature, darkness consumes

this space—a light dusting that insulates
its host. As countless as sand grains

that cover the continent, so too is this
dusted darkness that chafes her human grain

to reveal how she doesn't belong here.
Once her eyes adapt to this novel darkness,

she notes how shadows shuffle to stay
warm & stir circulation, how stillness slinks

over loose floorboards to seek ways out.
Her memories are frozen moments trapped

in hollowed labyrinths whose echo chambers
misfire recall in flittered metallic hiss

& crackle frequencies—their electrical
interference an untuned radio station's static

chaos. As she channels her inner calm, the earth
rumbles buried murmurs until it breaks

open discernment's flood gates, baptizing
without discrimination, drowning her

in fear. Unlike—or maybe, quite like—moths,
she can't handle small, dark places. Can't

breathe in this sheath that left her vulnerable,
not protected to weather this warped reality.

Unlike moths—whose wings can grate
rough planks until they find cracked

openings in this pine box cell to escape
captivity—she's bound in this tomb.

Her mounting anxiety, now the imago
whose static chaos claws until it tears

the veil & illuminates her metamorphosis
as lightning does a landscape with a flash

that bursts her mind into a bouquet of moths
rushing in a coiled swarm toward the light.

Into the Desert Empire

1.

She steals money from your savings to book a trip for two
to Coachella. Twelve days post-brain-op, she speaks
in mythical mysteries. Like the masters she has to see
at the festival of festivals, she's a legend—part natural
phenomenon, part Frankenstein's monster. She flies
to Cali for the first time. Meets middle sister at LAX after
first flight cancels, she misses second & has delays on third.

2.

She & sister Elis bicker like they did as kids. Elis was smart
enough to secure a tent, sleeping bags & air mattress before
they're dropped at their campsite in the middle of the desert.
Batteries for the mattress, however, were a rookie oversite.
Tia's erraticism mixed with Elis's irrational reaction to it
blends into toxic oxygen no one around them can inhale.

Their uber drops them & their bags off at Coachella,
not the campsite. They're two girls with more baggage than
even the guest services guy with his golf cart can handle.
In this heat he drops them at the venue campground despite
them showing him their offsite destination address.
They curse each other out for trusting him & for waiting
to buy water at the festival as they lug their luggage
a mile back to the gates, where their new uber waits.

3.

The sisters discover they have more fun when they split
up. Like they were in high school, they're solo drifters
whose survival relies on not letting others in far enough
to see behind the designer shades & boho threads.

Their fights are now contained to text threads they share
with you, forgetting their midnight rants reach you at 3am.

It's the witching hour & hours here dissolve quicker than pixie dust. The sisters morph to survive the Desert Empire. As Elis gets Insta-perfect shots by the Ferris wheel backlit by Cali's electric sunset, Tia secures a spot to watch the wild ones collect.

4.

Partially shaved head, too thin like the rest of them, Tia sneaks into the celebrity VIP booth. Her severe cheek bones make her almond eyes pop anime-style. Lounged back, cell at her hip, she snapchats Bieber bopping by. He's childlike small despite his larger than life status. Small, like she now knows she is under this canopy of star covered night. Bieber's third pass, he looks her way. She smiles & doesn't conceal her intrigue of his intrigue with her or his paranoia she's seen through his ruse. He fumbles with his phone at his ear, pretends to talk, but who'd hear him over SZA center stage?

She spots Bella Hadid. A Kardashian. Hailey Baldwin. DJ Khaled, filling two seats. Someone points out Rihanna in snakeskin pants, pussycat kill! sweater & Gucci ski mask.

When The Weeknd starts his set, Hadid slinks into shadows. Bieber's back to bop-walking the length of the box. He freezes as Tesfaye chokes during "Call Out My Name." He can't get through "when times were rough, when times were rough." Tia puzzles Gomez's choice to be with this awkward kid over the sweat-glistened man on stage. It's all child's play in this celebrity pen. Who's not noticing whom? Secretly watching whom? Who gets best dressed? The fairest

of them all? *What do any of them know about rough times?* She fits these last puzzle pieces into place in her mind.

For a little longer, she's one of them. Others snap shots of her. Some with her. Whisper about which celeb is hiding under that Navajo wrap. She hits her pen a few more times. Why let your buzz fade when you're surrounded by unicorns?

Escape Artist

In an old-money town overflowing
with trendy restaurants, she drives
an hour to the next big town to waitress.
Since her shifts were slashed in half
after returning to work, she's taken on
side jobs. This new one, she tells you,
offers her something she can't get
locally. She reads between your creased
brows & knows you don't buy it.

What? she demands, a quarrel brewing
behind her rolling eyes. *I have friends there*,
you reply. *Maybe they know the place.*
Don't worry. Your friends don't go there,
she laughs. *A gentlemen's club?* you ask.
My God, Mom! You always think
the worst. She knows you're thinking
sleezy bar & skimpy outfits but also knows
the first one to speak next will lose this
round. You'll never understand her
quest for such secrecy with you. *Well?*

She's shapeshifted into that same image
of the clever escape artist her teenage
self believed she was. She casts that look
she did when you caught her in a lie
but let her off the hook to swim
in her own folly. *As long as you pay me*
back, you lure the conversation back
to what you know you can control.

Sucker Punch to Your Gut

Have you seen this? Tia texts your 4-way
group chat. The pics are of the glowing new
girlfriend of her ex. *Wow, that was fast,*

Ang, the youngest, fires back. *Daaammn,*
Elis adds, *she's real slick. How many months
they been a thing?* Tia replies, *only a few.*

New news for me is all you think to say
in reply. *It's crazy,* she reasons. *i'm so over
him. we were toxic together that 2nd year.*

i don't know why this hit me so hard.
Because, you text, *you once imagined
yourself carrying his baby. It can't be*

that, she adds, *i don't want that anymore.*
so why does this hurt so bad? You measure
your words wisely before typing them.

*It's like everything else happening
for those around you while your own life
is on hold. It's a sucker punch to the gut*

*that takes your breath away when you're
already winded & knocked down.*

Face It

You're not in denial about your daughter's mortality
stats, nor the idea you'll likely outlive her.

Like the other insights that plague you, you've turned
this idea into a book not yet written for the world

outside your mind. You've dog-eared pages to revisit
once some psychic distance makes reading her

lifeline predictions a two-part act without tears.
A few years ago, her palmistry chirology foretold

a split lifeline—one shortened, though you don't put
faith in soothsayers & warned her not to mess with

mystical notions. You know there's more wisdom
in self-prophecy & speaking life over life matters

or not speaking about them at all. You tell yourself,
We're all in a moment without guarantee of the next.

Like this book you haven't committed to the page
yet, you bury your fears at the back of the bookshelf

with the other important works you know you must
carefully read but haven't time or energy for yet.

Yin & Yang

You sit, mother & daughter, planning an advance
directive. Except the daughter here is the patient,

the twenty-one-year-old patient. You discuss a tough
part about when to pull the plug when your wrist vibrates

with an email notification. editor@publishingco
. . . *Dear poet, I'm pleased to say . . . Wait,*

you say, the lump in your throat swelling. *I just landed
a book deal. Yes,* the message continues, *I enjoyed*

your manuscript & want to publish it. A book deal
—finally—your first one. The good & bad news

clash. & isn't that life's way? Your mourning delays
with celebrations & your celebrations with mourning?

You take a moment to celebrate & then return
to the paperwork needed for tomorrow morning's

craniotomy. You drift all day between worlds.
One you dread you must enter with your child.

The other world, one you waited a lifetime to enter.

Your Call

Between my prognosis & your poor health, she tells her father over the phone, *you know we'll probably die around the same time & Mom will outlive us all.* He can't imagine where this is headed. *What's wrong with you?* he asks. *I've been thinking about my frozen eggs & having babies only for me to die when they're still young. You don't know that,* he says. *Dad, we both know it's likely. Do you think it's selfish to still have kids? No,* he says. *Do you think Mom will mind raising them when I'm gone?* He doesn't want to imagine this outcome but says, *No, you know Mom would do anything for you.*

Out of Practice

Her childhood bedtime ritual went like this:

> she picked the book & you read it twice or
> it didn't count. Some lines stuck in your mind
>
> long after story time, lines like

- *I do not like them here or there.*
  I do not like them anywhere.[2]

- *Do you like my hat? I do not*
  like your hat. Goodbye. Goodbye.[3]

- *Chicka chicka boom boom,*
  will there be enough room?[4]

- *You'll miss the best things*
  if you keep your eyes shut.[5]

Still, she squeezed her eyes shut when she leaned in
to kiss you g'night. Wrapped her arms around your neck

& pressed her chest to yours. The hug didn't count
if it lasted less than a minute or if you didn't comb

your hands along each other's arms on the release.
She'd say, *I love you next to God & Jesus*

& everything in heaven—said this because
when she said, *I love you more than everything*

in the universe, you told her she couldn't love you
more than God. She followed this with, *I love you*

more than blankie, which was her entire world & you
wondered how long you'd hold this spot. *Love you more*

than blue moon with Sanders hot fudge, you'd reply.
& caramel, she'd add, awed she beat your favorite treat.

You honored this liturgy until junior high, inventing
new things to love each other more than, adding prayer

requests before the hug. Then this ritual was reserved
for rough times where your love & hugs were still the best

cure. When she moved, video calls replaced hugs,
though her blankie was still near her chin when it's time

to say g'night. She'd grin, sharing where you now fell
on her love list. One night, you said, *Let's pray for you*

tonight. You pray, she said, *God stopped listening to me*
                               & my prayers a long time ago.

Forgotten Prayer

Sparrows scar the sky with lost scripture
until morning falls upon your small town.

You eat dust kicked up by passing cars
as if it were communion meant to fuse

your daughter's broken brain. But nothing
mends her ionized mind now
                                    so severed

from her weathered heart, which dared
once to believe she ever stood a chance.

The Cancer Radiation Center

sits in the bowels of the medical building.
Ammonia masks the scent of rotting flesh
as drained patients head beneath ground level
for daily treatments. Dimly lit hallways lead
patients & their rides to a dimmer lit waiting

room dressed in canvas prints of bleeding hearts,
stargazer lilies & peonies, unfolding their satin hands
from a long night in prayer. It's always twilight here
in this underground world, casting every need

in shadows, amplifying their size. Dare you
unfold your own enwrapped hands—loose
your hold on faith seeds you've sown

as your daughter walks through this death valley
believing she'll emerge cleansed & unwilted?

Neuroplasticity

Art enables us to find ourselves
and lose ourselves at the same time.

—Thomas Merton

Post-brain-op, synaptic connections remap her
memories & identity. Her synaptic cleft
marks a new path that activates receptors
where related neurons connect to form
neural networks with thousands of links
that become uncharted footpaths
leading to lasting—& hopefully unearths
lost—memory. As her brain heals,

she relearns how to channel her emotions,
how to navigate flight-or-fight responses,
how to let love back into a dark place
now covered by cobwebs & chained
shut by derailed desire. Memory flickers,
flashes a key she's sure will unlock
her imagination before it becomes static
nothingness. Her art was once her escape.

Now it's an apparition—a phantom oasis
where calm & joy are a body of potential
water waiting to tame her chaos. In more ways
than she wants to count, she's returned
to grade school, especially her creative skills.
Your own artist ways & escapes offer insight
into how deep your daughter's loss runs.

This loss is a dry riverbed, refusing to open
a window the cruel earth has sealed shut.

Her Standpoint, a Completed Cubist Portrait of Mania

Manic moment.
      Moment in. Moment *in* a
          moment in.
      Time.
      Roads diverge and roads dissect. Dissect roads,
      diverge. Silence.
      Silence in. Silence within silence. Still
      silence and silence stills within a moment.
      Void.
Negate. Activate the frame by negating it.
      Negation.
Negation is a mirror.
Add smoke. (puff) Smokescreen puff of smoke, puff. (puff) (puff)
      Lungs.
      Lungs are to brain what time is to
moment. Brain.
      Brain pain. Brain strain. Brain games
running out of time. About time. There's
something
to be said about timing. Something some   thing.
      Hand.
The hand on the hand the other hand. On the other hand,
timing. Is something or is nothing, but something.
      Epiphany!
      Position is emotional. Position is an emotional
place absent of time within space, confined.
      Opposition. Happiness.
The key. The key to happiness is. The key to happiness is the key.
Lock. Those who pick locks gain.
Those who pick locks gain keys, long forgotten keys.
      Forgotten.

Forgotten is key. Key is to lock what time is to moment.
Take a moment. One point,   a spec.
Take a stand. Stand down. Stand still.
Stand. Standpoint. Her standpoint. New
wilderness ~~viewpoint~~. No.
New wilderness
               standpoint.
Let me recite what mania teaches. Mania teaches.[6]

Know a Person

There are a thousand things I could say
& for this reason, I choose to say nothing.

—Personal Proverb

During radiation + chemo, she picks up shifts to cover her disability deficit. Does this before she's added back to the schedule—though now only part-time. Her limitations are a nuisance to the ward & ignored by the charge nurse who sets up rounds. She toughs out shifts & survives most of them, finding clever ways to purge her gut contents between rounds & ice her head to fight the aches that send her home early. Though she spares the details of her moment-to-moment struggles, her worn pallor, receding hairline & scar invite clarity. *Brain cancer*, she offers, *with a side of radiation + chemo*. Each shift a new nurse, tech, doc, or patient tells her they know someone who had cancer, who, through treatment,

- never missed a day of work after surgery
- worked 2 jobs & didn't miss a beat during treatment
- didn't have restrictions or show signs of weakness
- never even let on they were suffering
- not once puked from chemo or even got nauseous
- had the worst cancer case & never complained
- kept the best attitude the entire time

She wonders why it's a competition among individuals since most cancer patients she knows are in solo fights for their lives, beating cancer their resolute focus. She wonders how many have spent time in the cancer treatment ward where zombies are walking dead versions of their former, glorious selves, scratching to escape from the weakened shell moving them through this hell on earth.

We're All Dying

someone says to her as she waits for her smoothie—
the only food she keeps down by week three.

She nods her head. *We're all dying*, she agrees.
She traces the surgical scissors in her scrubs pocket,

then the paper cutout of her ghost self she cut
from a recent nightmare. On a break between rounds

she cuts little accessories & uniforms for this doll
version of herself. She dresses her in a pink V-neck

& scrub pants. Pink: the only shade that won't wash
out her grey pallor. Last week, someone wrote

NEEDS TO SUCK IT UP & GET OVER IT
ALREADY on a message pad near the nurses' station.

She cuts these into dialogue bubbles & glues them
to toothpicks from her smoothie's strawberries.

DIE ON MY OWN TERMS she writes, then cuts
this into a thought bubble to add to the collection.

The Truth Is

You've mastered all the expected responses.

When people ask how your daughter's doing,
you say, *much better, her brain is healing,*
thank God, she's in remission, cancer free.

But the truth is she's a hot fucking mess.

You promised yourself you wouldn't swear
but you're out of kind words to describe her
erratic—worse than her teenage self—antics.

Recently, you got a call from someone worried
about a tweet that showed her holding a spoon
loaded with a filmy paste, cracking what

she calls a joke to drive traffic to her page.

Before that, it was ass shots & doe eyes.
Not that you're supposed to know any of this
or dare violate her privacy like a stalker mom.

She still thinks you're stupid, that you can't
tell what she's up to by filling in the details
she leaves out. You recently took a break

from following her secret media pages.
Sometimes you just can't see her that way
one more time. Then the crack pic call.

And it begins again. You're still paying for
her last teenage prank with sideways looks
& snarky remarks meant to remind you

your parenting failed to keep your kid in line.

But she's no longer a teenager, though
her brain has traveled back a few years.
Watching her self-destruct is a full-time job.

The truth is, if you'd remained a stay-at-home,
work-from-home mom, maybe you could
still micromanage her actions & moods—

hell, if you're speaking truths, she's never
been manageable. It's more like you're air-
traffic control & she's hijacked a plane

she has no idea how to navigate or where
to take. While you work to ground her,
she flies higher & faster, near missing

or clipping anything that gets in her way.
Lately, she's more like a rogue radical
whose mission is to fulfill some higher

call for a misinformed afterlife where
she'll be rewarded for her martyrdom
according to the destructive wake

she ignites in her final glory ride.
The truth is you want better for her.
Here it is, the truth you couldn't see

beneath her self-sabotage: she believes
she's unworthy of anything better.

Triangulated Path

God speaks to you
> through Red-tailed Hawks.

These winged messages are a sky-
> drawn lifeline. This morning

He showed you there are big fish in small
> ponds like the trout in your marsh

out back where wildlife has returned
> after too many deserted years to count.

Last week a hawk rose above the pines—
> a limp snake surrendered

in its sealed beak. He speaks
> to you in riddles, in a new living

testament not meant for the world
> outside your mind. In the beginning

of this month, a scrawny Red-tailed
> Hawk perched on a power

line overlooking your small town—
> no corn or beans in the crops

below. Days before, a hawk circled
> overhead when you opened your eyes

after praying, begging God to show you
> a sign He hasn't given up on you.

What of the one that swooped, near
> missing your windshield when you braved

the land of the living again
        after near missing your own cancer

scare? What of the Red-tailed Hawk
        that swooped low overhead at dusk

when you worked late poolside—so low
        you mistook it for a bat

before its wind path raised your stray hairs
        & fanned your notebook

pages until they settled on your notes
        that read: *she can't be trusted*

when she's quiet. what's she hiding?
        Your hairs now raised

by your mama instincts, you tune into
        your private Twitter account

she hasn't yet found to block.
        You scroll back for weeks—

how has it been weeks since
        you last stalked her, you agonize

as you read the reckless trail
        she's recorded with tweets.

What the hell are you doing? you ask
        when she answers your Facetime

call. Her jaw clenches & eyes panic
        as she scrambles for calm.

What do you mean? she says. *You know*
        what I mean. Your clenched jaw

in perfect mimicry of hers. *Stop stalking*
    me! My life is my business.

She's four again, her baby face flashes
    practicing rebel. *You're not*

the boss of me anymore, she finishes
    as if this is finished.

I'll always have your back, you shake
    your head, *without judgment.*

You're not my boss, she cycles back.
    I'll do what I want.

You're right, I'm not your boss.
    But we're in a sisterhood now

until death. Sisters here don't let
    their own rush to their demise.

It's weeks before you speak again,
    this time to plan her next move—

the third in a year. The hawks appear
    now in pairs close to home.

Two females perch on opposite boughs
    of a barren oak at the center of a marsh

wasteland you pass on a long run through
    backroads. Backs to each other,

they don't budge as you jog by. You recall
    your last call when talk turned

to exploitation & how it's a path to trafficking.
    I know what I'm doing. It's good

money, she says. *I need to make money.*
          Don't worry. Her fake resolve, frail

as the emotions that cloud her days.
          Let me help you is met by silence.

This silence roots itself in your interactions.
          So you stay rooted to your faith

& the power in your silent prayers & psychic
          bond you share with the hawks.

In mating season the sky is a stage.
          Their choreographed dance begins

at dizzying heights where graceful circles
          spin into locked bills & talons tornados

rushing them back to earth where she leads
          them to the perfect branch to finish

their dance. Your daughter's dance career leads
          her to South Beach, then LA.

She flies to sister clubs in a triangulated path
          between her PA home, LA & Miami.

Says she's doing modeling, though
          you know better. The first time

she needs your help, she's trapped in
          Inglewood after escaping a foiled

abduction at her car rental pickup. The next
          time it's for a plane ticket home

because she's sick & needs Mama's care.
          It's another hawk mating season

later when she cracks & asks you to help her
        break her contract. Your bird's eye

view & spirit realm vision are what drew
        your girls back to the roost in crisis

times, what helped you sit in wait, knowing
        that though hope deferred sickens

the heart, fulfilled longing is a tree of life
        whose limbs reach to the heavens

where trinity divinity heals broken souls
        with spiritual (re)awakening & new life.

An Open Letter to Your Daughter(s)

Dear daughter(s),

You're worthy of better. You're not one booty shot away from finding that right guy. Nor one viral video share from being discovered by anyone who deserves what's behind that smile, those eyes, that mind, the winter skin you've worn through your life-death battles.

Truth is, the world's sold you a lie, caged you in a mind-trafficking ring I hope to free you from. It may seem like your reputation's never been worse, that you've nothing left to lose. But there's a freedom you've always chased like your life depended on it. Have you forgotten this quest or is this another surgically removed memory casualty?

I remember watching you inch out further onto the ash branches out back, then wait for the swaying to subside before you reached & pulled yourself to the end. You always believed you were a bird. Sparrow, crow, hawk: the great hunter, always prepared to take flight—for your wings to unfurl you.

Was your moment of breaking that time you misjudged the branch's strength to hold you? Are your fears tethered to freefalling again from the sky face-first onto unforgiving earth? If I tell you again you've not been given a spirit of fear, will you believe it? If I tell you all the reasons you're worthy of more, will you believe in yourself again?

The Easy Part

They tell you chemo is the toughest
recovery. That radiation's burn
will turn to scar long before treatment

cycles cease. They tell you, keep her
on her side when she sleeps—keep her
from drowning in her vomit.

They tell you your daughter's recovery
will take years, maybe longer.
That some things may be forever lost.

That her brain is now a soft-boiled egg—
her skull a fragile shell ill-fit
to take a modest hit.   Shit,

they don't tell you she'll slip
into a reckless version of her teen self.
Slip into sexual exploitation

you'll spend over a year fighting
to rescue her from—half this time cut
from her trust circle after you catch her

encouraging her teen sisters to waitress
& bartend. You secretly stalk her
Twitter feeds from that account

she doesn't know to block. You
resist making every concern a battle.
If she knows where you get your facts,

she'll go private again. So, you pray
without ceasing—on your knees,
prostrate, in your car, while you work,

eat, fall asleep, through sleepless nights
& hazy days. Months into your prayers,
she's evicted from her rental home,

leaving you on the hook for back rent.
You meet her new *bae* on move out day.
After meeting you, he says he knew

someone invested in your daughter.
Knew she came from good folks.
That she's better than this persona

version of herself. This, he says,
is why he stuck around, spent so much
time helping her break free

from bogus contracts & fetish gigs
that would never earn her that big break.

Closing Time

You'll always see your daughter's new *bae*
as the one who discovered her

unconscious in a bathroom stall—her
legs outstretched beneath the door.

Someone had already killed
the lights during closing time rounds.

But he heard shallow breaths
as he made his final check.

Her head bent against the tile
wall meant she'd likely hit it

before blacking out. Just six months
after chemo & eighteen months

post brain-op, a blow to her head
could be fatal. He carried her

like a sleeping child to a back room
where their boss wouldn't see

one of his cocktail waitresses passed out
on her night off. She'd met a regular

for drinks—another bodybuilder,
though much older than this bouncer
who'd also been pursuing her

for weeks. He'd noticed the regular
leave without her hours ago. Assumed
she slipped out the back to escape

a bad date. Knew she hadn't even finished
the drink the guy bought her
because he rambled on about this fact

before closing his tab for the night.
When she came to, she didn't remember
anything after taking a few sips of her

Grey Goose & cranberry. She remembered
she'd left her bag with her meds
& money in the guy's car. He told them

the bag was his now when they came
to get it. Pointed a pistol at the storm
door that separated them. Said, *I hope*

you die in a ditch, nasty bitch,
homeless & alone. Then charged
through the door & fisted two rocks

from the landscape boarder. *This,*
he said, smashing granite back
into sand, *will be your heads*

if I see you again. She never saw
the money again but got her meds back
days later. Just weeks after this, he died

of a massive heart attack. He was alone
for days before a buddy found his body.

More Than a City on Fire

The thing is, you're "trying to smuggle her out of a burning city.
    Whatever you do, love, don't look back"[7] you tell her.
    Back home, four states away, you chart her new topography.
As you map elevations & steep terrain, she breaks ground in search
    of buried treasures. An entire forest blazes from her crazed eyes.
How do you classify this conflagration without limits, its desire
    to destroy, voracious? She's more than a city on fire—
more than a girl caught in a wildfire whose compass demagnetized.
    In place of a diurnal cycle, her internal gradient winds whirl,
    forecasting imminent fire storms that will devastate this
new landscape as they did the old. Her thoughts turn to foliage
    that canopies the fire's fuel source & changes the force of her
    inferno's convective column. In direct attack, she translates *don't
look back* into *don't look forward* as the rear of the fire smolders.

Give It More

Beyond briefing you on her advance directive
& the craniotomy, radiation & chemo risks,

no one tells you what parts of your daughter
will be forever lost. They don't tell you

her compassion will be the first casualty—
her best quality. Her patience cauterized

with the tumor tissues they send for biopsy.
Her creativity likely knit into the tumor

itself. You live in her 6 x 8 storage room
for eight weeks because you can't

rely on her roommates to manage her
post-op routines & treatment cycles.

Four states from home, you wonder
how much smaller you can grow,

how many more ways you can divide
yourself to meet all three daughters'

& your husband's needs. Almost three
decades ago, your husband survived

his own brain trauma. Lived but lost
his logic & bits of English—his second

language. Now quicker to anger & slower
to forgive, he's often a full-time job

when his mania's tripped or untreated.
Like with your daughter, they told you

he'd heal with time. Just give it more
time. But you know time alone

won't heal a broken brain. Won't
mend fractured lives which dared

to build their dreams on foundations
in landscapes with numerous faults.

New Puzzle

How long will you torment my soul,
and break me in pieces with words?

—Job 19:2

You rush to her again—race through
three states—on the four-year anniversary
of her brain surgery. Her dissociative mania,

a mirror image of her post-op psychosis.
You go because you know you're the one
she'll let in far enough to help her.

She can't stop talking on a digressive track,
can't finish a thought, let alone a story.
Your own focus derailed hours ago.

After two restless weeks, she sleeps. Not
from exhaustion. Rather, a drug-induced
slumber she fights until the fight pulls her

into a dream world she isn't ready to face
alone. In her first of many night   terrors,
she's alone on a platform between cities.

Did you think we'd hold the train for you?
the night watchman yells from the back
of the car as it wails away. Her mangled *yes*

transcends your own nightmare. This feral
plea escapes a place she allows no one
access. You try to find sleep   again

in the living room of her tiny apartment
you work two jobs to help her pay for
while she finishes anesthesia tech training.

The floor below creeks as you turn
side-to-side atop the air mattress wrecking
your already wrecked back. A backlash

breeze soughs down the hallway
from her bedroom's open window. In her
dream the ground sways; rumbles the corridor;

snuffs all other sounds. Ghost shadows
flicker across the platform. She breathes deep—
in for three, out for three, like you taught her.

She awaits the next train just as her therapist
instructed her. She enters the third car
when it arrives—three, like the Trinity

she calls upon for blood   protection.
For the test to work, she must tether herself
to the trap, must surrender   her thoughts.

The train enters an underground world,
an ocean world that circuits a shoreline
whose tide ebbs & pulls   something

away in jetsam scraps—scraps discarded
to lighten a vessel's load. Alone is the worst
time of day, especially in this dark place

where she loses herself in voids within
her own raging sea. Silence suffocates,
fetters her breath until she gurgles

her sewage memories. Memories of love
she lost because she was incapable
to return it. Visions of lost intimacy   & life.

She labors another in for three, out for three.
Focus, her therapist's reminder breaks
the silence. In for three, out for three.

In for three, out for three. She opens
her eyes outside the train, watches herself
through the glass pressed by thought.

She knows the interior of that look, knows
it like the blind know their living spaces.
Her eyes, a freshly trapped   animal

in a hunter's snare. The station lights flicker
as the train pulls away. Alone again,
she's assailed with guilt, with regret,

with everything taken away from her
without warning. Everything in the car
is underwater when the train returns.

She hugs herself, wishes she could hug
the self trapped in the train. Deformed
body parts of the baby never to be born

orbit the car just as their unformed parts
endlessly sink in her now vacant womb.

She doesn't know when the others entered
the corridor or why she's more   alone
on this populated platform. She stands

with these strangers who reasonably go
about their business, their heads cast
down the track as the next train enters

the station. The third car is   empty
when it stops. The others rush to enter
once the doors slide open. They slush

through her grief as it flows past them
& settles debris at her feet. Her therapist

was right: psychic distance separates self
from trauma. But grief is a rock-filled
pocket that helps floodwaters drown you.

Just as she entered this nightmare, she runs
from the station like a starved dog whose mission
was fouled by a swifter creature. Despite her

tearless recounting, her eyes cannot shield her
refreshed fears. Your own grief aside, you nurse
her through the hormone-triggered delirium

until you must leave her—again—to return
to your own life. Instead of rejecting you
like she did when you were her caregiver

during chemo + radiation, she holds you
close as if letting go of your prolonged hug
will splinter her madness into

the five-thousand-piece puzzle you spent
years piecing into a recognizable image of her
wilderness. She watches you from behind

the glass door to her building as you pull
away from the lot. She's a toddler again,
holding her stuffed puppy to her chest.

She blows you kisses & waits for you
to catch them, slap them on your cheek
& send kisses back. She seizes these,

then eats them so they can greet the unspoken
words you shared now trapped in her throat

as if your love is all she needs to fuse her
shattered soul into a new puzzle piece.

Notes

1. From "Only Happy When It Rains" by Garbage.

2. From *Green Eggs and Ham* by Dr. Seuss.

3. From *Go, Dog, Go!* by P. D. Eastman.

4. From *Chicka Chicka Boom Boom*, written by Bill Martin, Jr. and John Archambault, illustrated by Lois Ehlert.

5. From *I Can Read With My Eyes Shut* by Dr. Seuss.

6. From "If I Told Him, A Completed Portrait of Picasso" by Gertrude Stein: "Let me recite what history teaches. History teaches."

7. From "Notice Me" by John Rybicki.

Acknowledgments

A special thanks to Catrina, to whom this book is dedicated, and to my other loves, Nick, Elisabeth, and Angelina, who complete the cast of unruly characters in my life. To Lisa J. Sullivan, my trusted poet sister, whose insights and curiosity helped move this from a chapbook to a complete collection. And to Cornerstone Press for believing in this body of work, especially director Dr. Ross K. Tangedal and editors Maria Scherer and Brett Hill.

Gratefully acknowledged are the following publications, where particular poems appeared in earlier forms.

"After the Rain," "A New Wilderness," "Braiding Your Daughter's Hair After Brain Surgery," "Red Tide at Dusk," "[Re]Naming Things," and "Small, Dark Spaces" first appeared in a Tupelo Press 30/30 Challenge.

"After the Rain" appears in *Glacial Hills Review*.

An excerpt from "An Open Letter to Your Daughter(s)" appears in *Aurorean*.

"Asylum" appears in *Solstice*.

"Braiding Your Daughter's Hair After Brain Surgery" appears in *CALYX*.

"Detroit Institute of Arts" appears in *Mom Egg Review*.

"Forgotten Prayer" appears in the *Underground in America* anthology.

"Give It More" appears in *Pink Panther Magazine*.

"Neuroplasticity" appears in *Medical Literary Messenger*.

"Red Tide at Dusk" appears in *Last Leaves*.

"Surfing Darkness" appears on the Oakland University English Channel.

JENIFER DeBELLIS, M.F.A., is the author of *Warrior Sister, Cut Yourself Free from Your Assault* (2021) and *Blood Sisters* (2018). She edits *Pink Panther Magazine* and directs the a*RIFT*+ Warrior Project and the Detroit Writers' Guild (501c3). She's featured in *Psychology Today* and Seattle's *My Independence Report*, and her writing appears in *CALYX, The Good Men Project, Medical Literary Messenger, Solstice*, and elsewhere. A former Meadow Brook Writing Project fellow, JDB facilitates summer workshops for Oakland University and teaches at Saginaw Valley State University.

www.ingramcontent.com/pod-product-compliance
Lightning Source LLC
Chambersburg PA
CBHW031243120626
46545CB00007B/2630